BUSY TIMES

My Busy Year

Clare Hibbert

Illustrated by Silvia Raga

Evans

Published by Evans Brothers Limited
2A Portman Mansions, Chiltern Street, London W1U 6NR

© Evans Brothers Limited 2011
Concept devised for Evans Brothers by Clare Hibbert

Educational consultants: Sue Palmer, Josephine Hussey
Editor: Clare Hibbert
Designer: Sandra Perry
Illustrator: Silvia Raga (Milan Illustration Agency)

British Library Cataloguing in Publication Data

Hibbert, Clare, 1970-
My busy year. -- (Busy times)
1. Year--Juvenile literature. 2. Special events--Juvenile literature.
I. Title II. Series
529.2-dc22

ISBN-13: 9780237542658

Printed in China by New Era Printing Company Ltd.

The website addresses on page 22 are correct at the time of going to print but the publisher
cannot be held responsible for changes to website addresses or content.

Contents

Birthdays come just once a year. Mine's in winter, when it's cold outside. When's yours?

Party!

balloon

In spring we see ducks
and ducklings on the
pond in the park.
I spot some baby
swans, too.

Springtime

swan

duck

raincoat

wellies

Easter's a spring festival. People give chocolate eggs.

7

On hot summer days, Mum
gets out the paddling
pool. It's a fun way
to cool down.

Warm weather

cat

tea cup

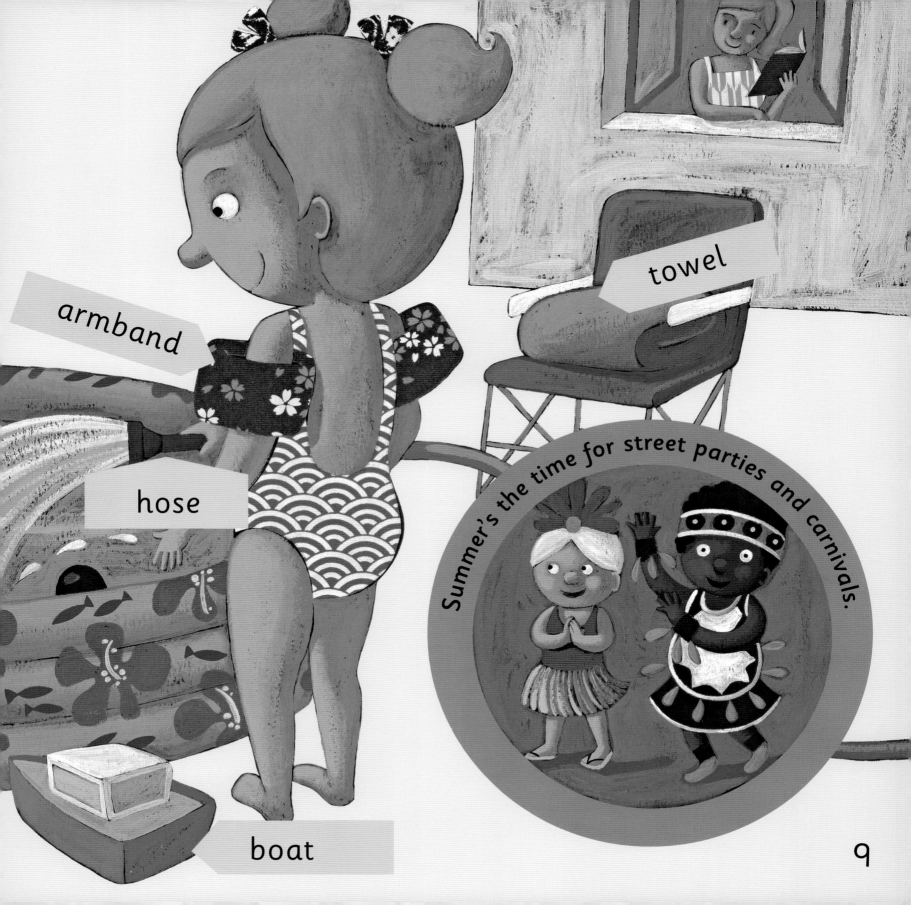

armband

towel

hose

boat

Summer's the time for street parties and carnivals.

9

I race with my classmates at sports day. Everybody cheers when we cross the finish line.

Sports day

T-shirt

finish line

teacher

plimsolls

Mrs Brown is putting out the drinks and snacks for when we finish.

In the holidays, we go to the seaside with some friends. We build sandcastles.

Summer holiday

picnic basket

deckchair

sandcastle

spade

bucket

Crabs live on the beach all year round.

13

In late summer Nana asks me to help her in the garden. There are lots of ripe vegetables.

Harvest time

onion

pumpkin

tomatoes

fork

carrot

basket

The farmer in this combine harvester is busy gathering wheat.

15

In autumn I like jumping about in piles of fallen leaves. I collect some of them to make pictures with.

Falling leaves

swallow

squirrel

16

tree

My friend Abdul is having a feast for Id.

17

The best thing about winter is snow. We build snowmen and make snow angels.

Snowy days

snowball

glove

snow angel

In winter people go skating at the outdoor ice rink.

19

At the end of the year
my class puts on a play.
It's about the first
Christmas, when
Jesus was born.

Christmas

wise
men

shepherds

20

Joseph

angels

Mary

Jesus

sheep

This month my friend Gabe celebrates Hanukkah.

21

Notes for adults

The **Busy Times** series links in to the Early Years Foundation Stage curriculum and beyond. The series provides useful resources for exploring time in accordance with the Early Years Foundation Stage Practice Guidance from birth to five.

In today's fast-paced world, it's more important than ever to talk with young children about the passage of 'real time'. Television programmes, films and games often confuse children – for example, by using cutting techniques that telescope time passing.

The series supports young children as they begin to grasp the complex concept of time. It looks at how we mark specific moments, and how children can come to predict the order of routine events. Although children do not tell the time at this stage, they will enjoy hunting for the hidden clocks and watches.

In order to introduce the passing of time in an age-appropriate way, every spread in the **Busy Times** books illustrates a moment in a child's day, week, year or life.

As you explore the books together, you can use the pages to link in with the specifics of the child reader's life. Discuss what he or she does at those particular times. Which settings are familiar favourites? Which activities are new or unfamiliar?

Each spread also has a unique 'Window on the World' feature. Through this, children can glimpse something else happening at the same time as the main action on the spread – another, concurrent event. The window is really useful for broadening children's perspective, helping them to understand that things go on even when they are not there.

USEFUL WEBSITES

Department for Education	www.education.gov.uk
National Literacy Trust	www.literacytrust.co.uk
Early Years resources	www.earlyyearsresources.co.uk, www.underfives.co.uk

Reading with younger children

As you read, allow quiet spaces so that children can ask questions or repeat your words. Try pausing mid-sentence so that children can predict the next word. This sort of participation gives a sense of achievement and develops early reading skills.

Follow the words with your finger. The main text in the **Busy Times** books is in Infant Sassoon, a clear, friendly font designed for children learning to read and write. The sound effects add fun and introduce readers to different levels of communication.

Take time to explore the pictures together. Ask children to find, identify, count or describe different objects — not just the hidden timepieces. Point out colours and textures. The illustration style in the **Busy Times** series is especially rich and rewarding.

Children delight in repetition; they also need to revisit complex concepts on a regular basis. Expect to share these books time after time. There is lots of scope in the pictures for many different conversations.

Use the Busy Year spreads as a springboard for extension activities:

• Practise saying the names of the months of the year together. Children love to chant and it's an effective way of getting the order of the names to 'stick'.

• Help children to make a birthday book or calendar. Use it as a prompt to sing 'Happy Birthday to You' to each child when his or her birthday comes around.

• Familiarize children with the seasons by asking them to photograph the same place — preferably somewhere with a tree — each month. Use the photos to gradually build a calendar frieze along a wall.

• Seasons lotto is a simple, four-player game. First, make a lotto card for each season: spring, summer, autumn and winter. Draw eight season-related images on each one. Copy each image on a small square of card. To play, place the card squares upside down. Players take turns to turn one over. If it matches an image on their lotto card, they put it on their lotto card. If it doesn't, they turn it back over and play passes to the next player. The first person to cover all the images on their card is the winner.

Index